THÉÂTRE DU CHATELET

Gran Teatre del Liceu

TEMPORADA OFICIAL DE PRIMAVERA DE 1934

THE PHIL...RUM

...rmance of the Season

by

Colonel W. de Basil's
BALLETS RUSSES

THÉÂTRE DES CHAMPS - ÉLYSÉES

15, avenue Montaigne

Boston Opera House

LEE and J. J. SHUBERT, Proprietors

SAINT LOUIS
SYMPHONY
SOCIETY

Presents

AUDITORIUM THEATER
CHICAGO

GEORGE A. KINGSBURY
MANAGING DIRECTOR

TELEPHONE
HARRISON 6554 & 5000

ORPHEUM
THEATRE
A MORT H. SINGER THEATRE

SIOUX CITY, IOWA

SOCIEDAD FILARMÓNICA
DE VALENCIA

SOCIEDAD FILARMONICA

VALENCIA

CHARING CROSS
ROAD
LONDON, W.C.2

THE
ALHAMBRA
THEATRE

LEICESTER
SQUARE
LONDON, W.C.2

PROGRAM
PUBLISHED
BY THE
NEW YORK
THEATRE
PROGRAM
CORPORATION

NRA

ST. JAMES THEATRE

44th STREET WEST OF BROADWAY
DIRECTION LODEWICK VROOM
BOX OFFICE, LAC. 4-4664 — OFFICE, PEN. 6-3231

THE BALLETOMANE'S SCRAP-BOOK

Australia and New Zealand
THE OXFORD UNIVERSITY PRESS, MELBOURNE

South Africa
THE OXFORD UNIVERSITY PRESS, CAPE TOWN

India, Burma, China and F.M.S.
MACMILLAN AND COMPANY, LIMITED
BOMBAY   CALCUTTA   MADRAS

THE BALLETOMANE'S SCRAP-BOOK

BY

ARNOLD L. HASKELL

AUTHOR OF 'BALLETOMANIA,' ETC

WITH 193 ILLUSTRATIONS

A. & C. BLACK, LTD

4, 5 & 6 SOHO SQUARE, LONDON, W.1

1936

MADE IN GREAT BRITAIN.
PRINTED BY HARRISON AND SONS, LTD.,
LONDON AND HIGH WYCOMBE

INTRODUCTION

This is nothing more than a scrapbook, a souvenir of the work and life of Colonel de Basil's Russian Ballet, from its formation in 1932 till the present day. I have selected from many thousands of photographs those that I personally would like to have with me were I marooned on a desert island far from all ballet. Some of the scenes depicted are trivial, perhaps they are too personal in their appeal, but it is just those pictures of relaxation that are never published that have interested so many people in my private scrapbook. However, there is sufficient of a record of the actual ballets to compensate, if necessary, for these few souvenirs of idle hours.

I have in my collection countless photographs of the past, including one such album as this published in Russia many years ago, when the words *Imperial* Ballet still had a meaning How old-fashioned and stilted many of these photos seem. My friend Prince Wolkonsky, former director of the Imperial Theatres, has remarked how much better the modern dancer poses for her photograph. Did it merely seem so to him or will many of these pictures too also provoke smiles in thirty years time? As a document then its publication will certainly be fully justified.

I have let the photographs tell their own story, with just a few notes of explanation and identification. Yet, I have arranged them so that they tell a story, not only of the formation and the subsequent triumphs of one company, but of the grounding of ballet in a great tradition that continues from generation to generation, uninterrupted by the death of individuals however great. These children who are growing before our eyes, who have enjoyed a success hitherto unknown to anyone so young in the history of ballet, are still far from perfect, perhaps it is a part of their charm that they are learning daily on the stage and that we can measure that progress from season to season. In spite of their imperfections, however, already they belong to the main history of Ballet, the history that includes the giants, Taglioni, Elssler, Zucchi and Pavlova. They have created important works and, what is more important still, they have earned the right to do so, for their artistic pedigree is faultless. Dancing is essentially an aristocratic art, and these young dancers can trace their method back through their teachers Preobrajenska, Kchesinska, Egorova, Trefilova and Volinine to the very origins of the classical dance at the court of Louis XIV, and the tradition has not passed through so many hands for dancers are long lived. The true measure of their greatness will be whether they can enrich that tradition, whether in their turn they can hand down, as their teachers have done, more than they themselves have received.

The dedication to Colonel de Basil is more than either an act of friendship or of formal politeness. To him we owe to-day the tremendous vogue of ballet both in England and America. He has created a vast public, and he has encouraged in his company both English and American dancers. He has had faith in the young and untried, he has had the courage to combat the scepticism of others. He has set a standard of work that it will be difficult to equal and has so benefited the whole of our art.

Arnold L. Haskell.

London, 1936.

ACKNOWLEDGMENTS.

I am deeply indebted to MONSIEUR M. BARONOFF for over fifty photographs taken specially for this volume, and also to the many amateurs whose love of ballet has made them into excellent photographers.

Also the following must be acknowledged :—

GORDON ANTHONY, for Toumanova Interrupted ; Lubov Tchernicheva as Zobeide ; Danilova in The Good Humoured Ladies.

R. BARBA (of Monte Carlo), for Présages I, II ; Baronova and Lichine, Présages III ; Sylphides I, II ; Jeux d'Enfants I ; Beach I ; Sylphides IV ; Beau Danube I ; Scuola di Ballo II ; Carnaval I ; Firebird I, II ; Cotillon III.

BATTLES (of Barcelona), for Toumanova in Les Sylphides ; Toumanova and the Statue ; Aurora's Wedding I ; Grigorieva as Chiarina ; Grigorieva as an Odalisque ; Scheherazade III ; Baronova in Le Spectre de la Rose ; Jardin Public I ; Vanca Psota as Nicolo ; Prince Igor.

W. BREWSTER, for The Master of Ceremonies ; Beach II ; Scuola di Ballo I ; Scuola di Ballo III ; Choreartium Rehearsal.

STUDIO IRIS, for Preobrajenska and her pupils ; Kchesinska in her Studio ; Cotillon I ; Paris, St. Lazare ; Union Pacific I ; Danilova in Choreartium.

H. GLARNER, for Riabouchinska 1934 ; Union Pacific ; Massine's Dance ; Beau Danube II ; Miller's Wife and the Governor.

MAURICE GOLDBERG (N.Y.), for Traveller dances with the child ; Pas de Trois ; Petrouchka II ; Tricorne II ; Présages, the second tableau ; Présages V.

SACHA, for de Basil and Massine inspecting scenery ; Dress Rehearsal ; Delarova as Felicita ; In the wings, Covent Garden ; Boutique Fantasque II ; End of Season.

F. J. GUTMAN, for Les Cent Baisers II.

L. N. A., for Murder of the Prince ; Supper after première ; Irina Baronova after Première ; Gala at Covent Garden.

STAGE PHOTO CO., for Thamar I ; Thamar II.

LIPNITZKI, for Toumanova in 1929 ; Verchinina in Présages.

DAILY HERALD, for Toumanova in her dressing room ; Concurrence.

My Dear Vassili Grigoritch,

This record of your
Company since its inception is dedicated
to you not merely because it is yours
by right, but in souvenir of the many
journeys we have made together and in
anticipation of many more in the future.
I shall not readily forget a certain
dash by car from Monte-Carlo to Paris
with you at the wheel with a badly
poisoned hand, my fears, your songs,
our delicious meals en route and your
five p.m. radio concert. I have yet
to see you truly tired, hence the amazing
record of work, 1932-1935, celebrated
in this volume.

   Yours Arnold L. Haskell

To Colonel. W. de Basil

       London 1936

BALLET DID NOT DIE WITH HER

On January 23rd, 1931, Anna Pavlova died in the Hague. This showcase in a museum and
a fading memory of the Swan are not all that remain.

The greatest dancer the
world has seen, she continues
as an inspiration to every
young dancer to-day.

BALLET DID NOT DIE WITH HIM
In August, 1929, Serge de Diaghileff died in Venice.

The artists he inspired, the public h[e]
created, have remained to give birth to the
new.

WHILE
INDIVIDUALS DIE
BALLET CONTINUES

$\longrightarrow$

THE TRADITION INTACT: ARTISTIC PEDIGREES

The new movement in ballet starts in the studios of the great Maryinsky ballerinas in Paris, where Colonel de Basil and Georges Balanchine first saw some promising children. Olga Preobrajenska, great ballerina, is here seen as she appeared before the Saint Petersburg balletomanes, and as she is to-day with her two greatest pupils, Baronova and Toumanova.

Olga Preobrajenska in her famous sailor's dance, as much associated with her name as the Swan with Pavlova, the Russian dance with Kchesinska.

Irina Baronova, who arrived in Preobrajenska's studio via Petrograd and Roumania, seen here after her first six months at class.

Tamara Toumanova in 1929, aged ten, just before being invited to the Paris Opera as a guest artist.

LIPNITZKI
PARIS

Tamara Toumanova, aged 7, at the time she entered Preobrajenska's studio. She is one of the many thousands of little girls who had seen Pavlova, and who from that moment could dream of nothing else. In this case the dream took her from Shanghai to Paris, and she was fortunate in making her début at the Trocadero, during a Pavlova Gala, shortly after this snapshot was taken.

Tamara Toumanova in 1929. "Is she always 16?" a sceptical correspondent wrote to me. At one time it was found expedient to reverse the usual process and add a few years to her age.

L'EVENTAIL DE JEANNE
The ballet in which Toumanova (centre) appeared at the Paris Opera. It was written by ten composers in collaboration, one for each year of her age.

Mathilde Kchesinska, *ballerina assoluta*, the charming dictator of the St. Petersburg ballet, seen at the height of her fame and as she is to-day in her Paris studio.

Mme. Kchesinska is the Princess Romanovsky-Krasinsky, wife of The Grand Duke André.

Mathilde Kchesinska in her greatest role, Esmeralda, in which a pet goat appeared with her on the stage.

431.

Her pupil, Tatiana Riabouchinska, daughter of a dancer and half sister of the charming Diaghileff artist, Heléne Komarova.

HALT FOR REPAIRS

A dancer has never finished learning. However great her success, she is always the small unfinished pupil to her maitre de ballet.

Kchesinska correcting Riabouchinska after a long tour, during which classes have given place to rehearsals and travel.

Riabouchinska (1934)

LES PRESAGES (I)

After the Monte Carlo première, L. to R. : Serge Grigorieff, Tatiana Riabouchinska, Nina Verchinina, Irina Baronova, Colonel de Basil, René Blum and Leonide Massine.

Ballet by Massine on Tchaikovsky's 5th Symphony.   Decorations and Costumes by André Masson.   Choreography by Massine.

EARLY DAYS

The young company in th
Monte Carlo class roo
cradle of great dancers.

Toumanova, Lichine a
Riabouchinska.

LES PRESAGES (II)
Final Tableau : Triumph of the Hero.

The same tableau in its final
rehearsal before the Princess
of Monaco.

BARONOVA AND LICHINE

Recreation. The thirteen year old ballerinas, Toumanova
and Baronova, enjoying a swing (1932).

LES PRESAGES (III)
The Fourth Tableau
This was the ballet that largely contributed to make the company famous on its début at the Alhambra, London, July 4th, 1933.

Nina Verchinina as Action in Les Présages.

LES PRESAGES (IV)
The Second Tableau
Passion (Lichine) lifting Baronova

The Second Tableau
One of the lovers (Baronova) overpowered
by Fate (Woizikovski).

LES PRESAGES (V)

[Ba]ronova, as one of the lovers, [re]coils before the onslaught of Fate.

In a happier mood. Bitter rivals on the stage, Baronova and Toumanova enjoy a holiday together (1934).

Tamara Toumanova
Sylphides.

Ballet by Fokine.
Music by Chopin.
Decorations & Costumes
by Benois.
(in this version decorations
Prince Shervachidze)
Choreography Fokine.

LES SYLPHIDES (I)
The London season opened
with Les Sylphides.
Fokine's masterpiece has
proved so popular that in
1935 seven Companies per-
formed it in London.
According to the late André
Levinson, a severe critic,
Colonel de Basil's children
rivalled the famous nymphs
of 1912.

LES SYLPHIDES (II)

Seen from every angle it is completely
harmonious.

(*Above*) Riabouchinska dances the
prelude.

(*Below*) The Electrician's view.

MAKE-UP

and minute detail of costume are vital
in such a ballet as this, and Grigorieff
is a stern guardian of the traditions.
Baronova giving a last glance at an
hour's work before the mirror.

A REHEARSAL

In the famous Monte Carlo room where Diaghileff
deliberated, Fokine created, and Cecchetti taught.

Outside the artists are sitting
on the bench (L.-R.: Zorina,
Delarova, Danilova), known
to every dancer since 1910,
or eagerly reading the morning
mail (L.-R.: Bousloff, Danilova,
Haskell, de Basil, Sevastianov,
Mme. Baronova).

LES SYLPHIDES (III)

Danilova and a group. Fokine's handling of the corps de ballet here was considered revolutionary by the die-hard balletomanes, used to an almost military formation. These beautiful groups were actually set by him as a last minute thought before curtain rise. Diaghileff, whose favourite ballet it was, rightly said that there could be no corps de ballet, only a group of sensitive artists.

(*Left*) The Valse: Toumanova, Petroff, Baronova.

Ballet by Boris Kochno. Music b
Chabrier. Décor and Costumes, (
Berard. Choreography, George
Balanchine. Created 1932.

" The Master of Ceremonies
(Woizikovski) turns up late and in
a hurry." An opening scene from
Balanchine's masterpiece, a poem
that means little in description,
but that is deeply moving in
action. This was one of the first
ballets danced by the young company.

JEUX D'ENFANTS (I)

Massine's first ballet for the company (1932), a surrealistic version of Boutique Fantasque!
Riabouchinska as the Child watching the Amazons.   (Music, Bizet; décor, Miro; Book, Kochno.)

The Traveller (Lichine) dances with the
child (Riabouchinska).

Pas de trois : The Sportsman (Woizikovski), the
top (Baronova), The Child (Riabouchinska).

CONTES RUSSES

A revival of a war-time creation by Massine. Above are seen the Princess's ladies-in-waiting, below Riabouchinska as the little girl who is frightened by the wood sprites, and who saves herself by remembering to make the sign of the cross. She is also seen with Shabelevsky.

Music by Liadov. Décor and costumes, Larionov. Choreography, Massine.

allet by R. Kerdyk.
usic, Jean Françaix.
écors , Raoul Dufy.
Choreography,
assine. Created
1933.

BEACH (I)
The Rose Maid (Baronova) dances with the handsome swimmer (Lichine).
This work is a balletic glorification of Monte Carlo Beach.

ach " in real life
onova and Tchinarova).

Baronova at Eden Roc, 1934.

The oriental carpet seller tempts the bathers with
his wares.

TOUMANOVA INTERRUPTED AT REHEARSAL BY A BALLETOMANE

PARIS, ST. LAZARE

TO NEW YORK HARBOUR (1934)

On the theatre roof, Barcelona.

TRAVEL (96 towns in 7 months)

Train . . . theatre . . . train. To-day in Little Rock, Ark.; to-morrow in Kansas City, Mo. There is rest on the boat, but not for all. Massine prepares new ballets, the conductors study their scores, de Basil plans and cables, and some of the company practise (weather permitting).

Massine, Baronova, Sono Osato.

Massine in the caravan in which he tours.

LES SYLPHIDES (IV)

Les Sylphides has been danced under all circumstances : on board ship during a storm, in the narcissus fields in Montreux, and at an exhibition of art in Brussels.

Here are three examples.

In the theatre.

In the Bull ring, Mexico City.

In the Ballroom, Monte Carlo.

BEACH (II)

American sailors flirting with the pyjama girl: Massine (facing camera), Delarova and Woizikovski.

The same: Delarova, Woizikovski, Massine.

Empty seats, full house, Covent
Garden, midday.

Some hours later

Meanwhile in the theatre always rehearsal, from ten till one, from 3.30 to 5.30.

De Basil and Massine inspecting the scenery of Union Pacific. Has it been damaged during its many travels

Thank God for an English Sunday and for the kind friends who give us Zoo tickets, says the company, who have double work on Sundays in all other countries.

DRESS REHEARSAL

of La Boutique Fantasque.   Grigorieff is approached with a hundred and one problems, from the tracing
of a missing pair of shoes to a request for an advance.

Serge Grigorieff and Leonide
Massine at a rehearsal.

UNION PACIFIC (I)
Irina Baronova as the vamp, Lady Gay (heavily made up with an addition to her nose to conceal the friendly snub), charming the Chinese overseer, Paul Petroff.

And as a contrast Irina Baronova on a holiday—gay, but not Lady Gay.

UNION PACIFIC (II).

Leonide Massine in his inimitable barman's dance, a remarkable piece of Americana ; Vera Zorina (*right*) as the Mexican camp follower, watching the dance.

Libretto, Archibald Macleish. Music by Nabokoff. Scenery and décors, Johnson. Costumes, Irene Sharaff. Choreography, Massine. 1934.

UNION PACIFIC (III).
The Irish gang at work.

(*Left*) Vera Zorina as the Mexican girl.

In Mexico.

UNION PACIFIC (IV).
In the Big Tent, where the workers rest, meet
the ladies of the town, drink and brawl.

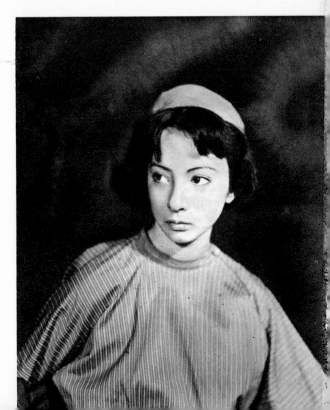

Sono Osato as the barman's assistant.
The Russian Ballet is by no means exclusively
Russian; it seeks talent from every country.
Perhaps Sono Osato is the first Japanese-
American Russian dancer.

TAMARA

Toumanova

TAMARA TOUMANOVA,
Black Pearl of the Russian Ballet.

A Russian balletomane once said, " Show me
her face and I will tell you if she can dance."
He was not far wrong ; charm is an essential,
beauty a strong asset.   The term " a plain
ballerina " seems an absurd contradiction.

MAKE-UP. (Irina Baronova.)
The eyes, a lengthy job, each lash being picked out first with ' rimmel ' and then increased in length by the application of blobs of hot wax.

The make-up finished : as the Princess in Children's Tales.

BEAU DANUBE (I).
The original version, 19
(Lopokova,   Marra   a
Massine).

This ballet was given at t
company's London premiè
It was composed by Massi
as a relaxation after "
Sacre   du   Printemps,"
tribute to the Viennese wa
during the height of the Ja
era.

The new version, 1933. T
street dancers (Danilova a
Borovansky).

"Beau Danube."   Music by
Johann Strauss. Décor and cos-
tumes by Polunin (after Guys).
Choreography, Massine. 1923.

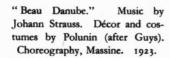

The Mazurka (Riabouchinska and Massine).

BEAU DANUBE (II).

Irina Baronova as the midinette.

" Scuola di
Comedy by Goldoni
ranged by Massine.
Boccherini.   Déco
costumes, Etienne de
mont.   Choreog
Massine.

SCUOLA DI BALLO (I).
Rosina (Riabouchinska) shows her talent

Rosina (Riabouchinska) dances with Carlito (Massine).

Tatiana Riabouchinska.

SCUOLA DI BALLO (II).
The scene is the dancing academy of Professor Rigadon.

SCUOLA DI BALLO (III).

Conclusion of the dance between Felicita (Delarova) and Don Fabrizio (Borovansky), an impresario.

Eugenia Delarova as Felicita, the impossible pupil.

Pas de Deux.
Riabouchinska and Massine as Rosina and Carlito.

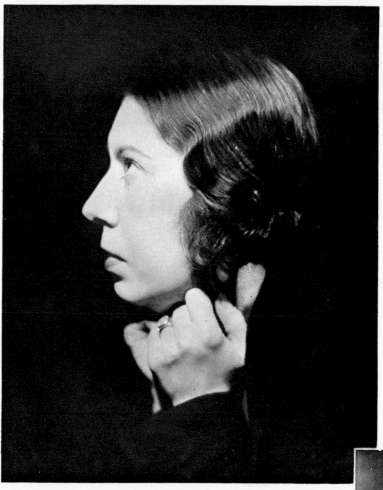

LA NIJINSKA.
Member of a famous family, great dancer and choreographer, creator of Les Noces, Les Biches, Hamlet, etc.

Irina Baronova after the première of "Les Cent Baisers" (1935).

Supper after the première of "Les Cent Baisers" (La Nijinska, Frederic d'Erlanger and Irina Baronova). Choreographer, composer and ballerina.

LES CENT BAISERS (I).
The Prince (Lichine) greets the Princess (Baronova) and offers his gifts—

while behind the scenes gifts from friends await the dancers at the curtain fall. At Covent Garden, 1935 season, the dancers received 1863 bouquets from their admirers!

"Les Cent Baisers." Ballet Boris Kochno, from a [sto]ry by Andersen. Music Frederic d'Erlanger. [Dé]cor and costumes, Jean [H]ugo. Choreography, La Nijinska.

LES CENT BAISERS (II).
The King (Borovansky), seeing the swineherd kissing his daughter, turns her out of doors.

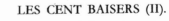

Pas de deux of the maids in waiting (Vera Zorina Tamara Grigorieva).

THE WARDROBE.

Serge Grigorieff superintending repairs. The damage caused by double work and heated dancers necessitates continuous work and great expense. This department is continually busy.

The Blue Bird's silk and jewelled jerkin in the making.

AURORA'S WEDDING (I).

Two interpretations of the most dignified and severely classical of all roles—Princess Aurora.

Irina Baronova,

Tamara Toumanova.

AURORA'S WEDDING (II).
A general tableau (Danilova as Aurora).

" Aurora's Wedding." One-act excerpt from " The Sleeping Princess." Music by Tchaikovsky. Décor, Bakst. Costumes, Benois and Gontcharova. Choreography, Petipa. Additional dances by La Nijinska.

(*In the wings*) A Duchess (Baronova) talking to the Blue Bird (Riabouchinska).

AURORA'S WEDDING (III).
(Baronova as Aurora.)
This brilliant *suite de danses* is all
that remains of the great five-act
ballet revived by Diaghileff at the
Alhambra in 1921.

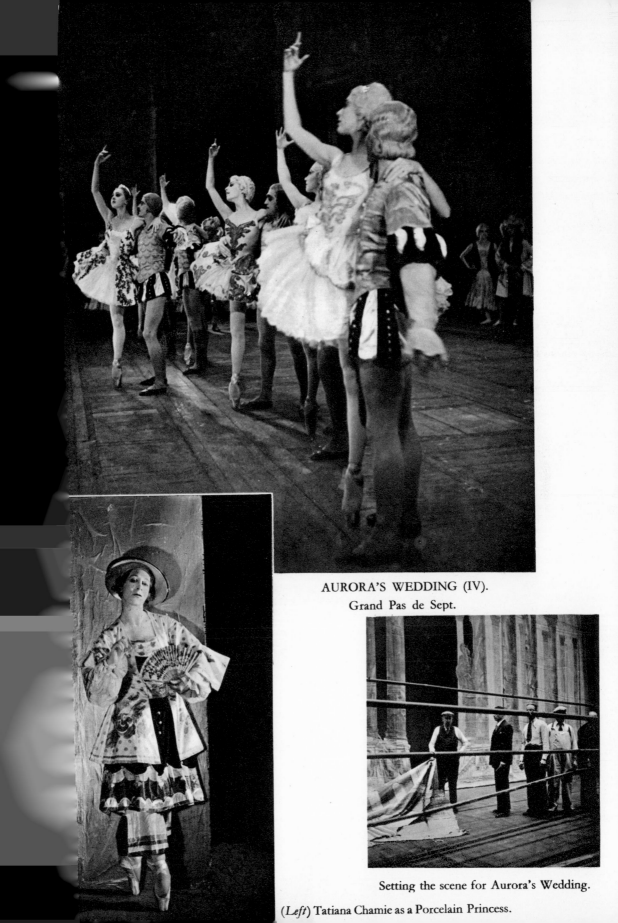

AURORA'S WEDDING (IV).
Grand Pas de Sept.

Setting the scene for Aurora's Wedding.

(*Left*) Tatiana Chamie as a Porcelain Princess.

CARNAVAL (I).
Tamara Grigorieva as Chiarina.

"Carnaval." One-
act ballet by Fokine.
Music by Schumann.
Décor and costumes,
Bakst. Choreo-
graphy, Fokine.

Fokine as Harlequin in
"Carnaval." (1912.)

In the wings, Covent Garden, during a performance of " Carnaval."

SCENE PAINTING.
Prince Shervachidze executing a décor, flat,
according to the Russian method.

One of the most popular of all ballets, it was performed in London by five different companies in 1935. Like many famous works by Fokine, it was originally performed at a charity performance in St. Petersburg.

THE FIREBIRD (I).   Wedding of the Prince.

" The Firebird."   Ballet by
Fokine.   Music by Stra-
vinsky.   Décor and cos-
tumes,   Gontcharova.
Choreography,   Fokine.
1910.

Property man retouching the grotesque masks used
in " The Firebird."

THE FIREBIRD (II).
In the enchanted garden.

David Lichine as Kastchei, the immortal.

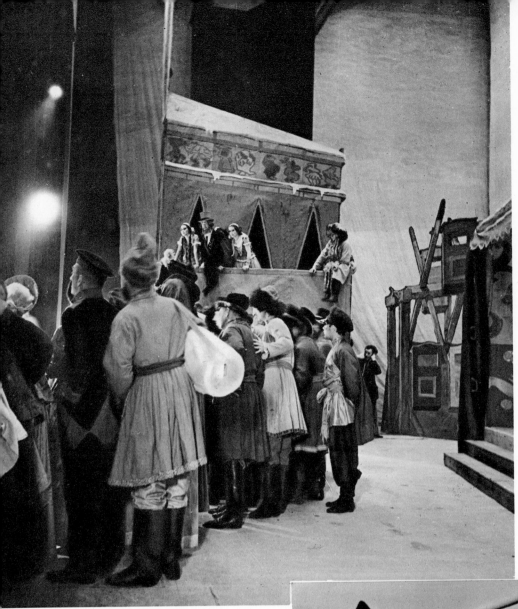

"Petrouchka."

Ballet by W. Benois and M. Fokine. Music by Stravinsky. Décors and costumes, Benois. Choreography, Fokine.

PETROUCHKA (I).
From the wings ; the fair in progress.

Alexandra Danilova as the dancer, a last minute look at make-up.

PETROUCHKA (II).

Tamara Toumanova as the dancer, Leon Woizikovski as Petrouchka. (*Inset*) " Sur les pointes," Tama
Toumanova.

SCHEHERAZADE (I).
Tamara Grigorieva
as an Odalesque.

This is the ballet that first made
Bakst's fame and launched a whole
period of bright colouring and the
exotic in decoration. Smart Paris
hostesses outdid one another in
giving Arabian Nights parties.

Scheherazade." Music by Rimsky-
Korsakov. Décor and costumes, Bakst.
Choreography, Fokine. First produced
1910. Revived 1935.

Zobeide (Tchernicheva) about to
betray the Sultan ; the eunuch is
unlocking the fatal centre door.

SCHEHERAZADE (II).   The Sultan (Grigorieff) takes leave of his wives.

Lubov Tchernicheva as Zobeide.

Serge Grigorieff in his make-up as
The Sultan.

SCHEHERAZADE (III).

Two interpretations of the slave " with the spring of a black panther."

LEONIDE MASSINE.

YUREK SHABELEVSKY.

BOUTIQUE FANTASQUE (I).
The toy Cossacks and the Mazurka dancer (Delarova). (*Left*) A real Cossack,
Colonel de Basil.

The Electricians during La Boutique
Fantasque.

BOUTIQUE FANTASQUE (II).

Music by Rossini (arr. Respighi.) Costumes and décor, Derain. Choreography, Massine.

Alexandra Danilova and Leonide Massine in The Can-Can.

BOUTIQUE FANTASQUE (III).
Dance of the Snob (Shabelevsky) and the Melon Vendor (Jan Hoyer).

THAMAR (I).

Thamar (Tchernicheva) and the Prince (Massine).   (A photograph taken at rehearsal.   Thamar's
famous headdress is missing.)

THAMAR (II). The Prince arrives.

" Thamar." Music by Balakeroff,
Décor and costumes, Bakst.
Choreography, Fokine.

Murder of the Prince.

LE SPECTRE DE LA ROSE (Irina Baronova and Paul Petroff).

Romantic reverie in one act by J. L. Vaudoyer, after the poem by Théophile Gautier. Costumes and décor, Bakst. Choreography Fokine. 1911.

Music by Weber.

" Soulève ta paupière close
Qu'effleure un Songe Virginal.
Je suis le spectre de la rose
Que tu portais hier au bal "

Irina Baronova.

Vera Fokine and Michael Fokine.

THE RICH COUPLE.
(Danilova and Petroff.)

THE POOR COUPLE.
(Toumanova and Massine.)

" Jardin Public " Scenario by Dukelsky and
Massine. Music by Dukelsky. Costumes
and décor, Lurçat. Choreography, Massine
1935.

ALEXANDRA DANILOVA
(in Choreatium and The Good Humoured
Ladies,)

The miller's wife (Toumanova)
and the Governor (Lichine).

Picasso's décor.

"Le Tricorne"

Ballet by Martinez Sierra, from a story
by Alarcon. Music, da Falla. Scenery
and costumes, Picasso. Choreography
Massine. 1919.

At curtain fall.

LE TRICORNE (II)

The miller and his wife
(Massine and Toumanova).

The miller's wife, the governor
and the miller (Toumanova,
Lichine and Massine).

LE TRICORNE (III).

Lubov Tchernicheva as the miller's wife.

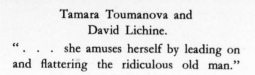

Tamara Toumanova and
David Lichine.

" . . . she amuses herself by leading on
and flattering the ridiculous old man."

LES FEMMES DE BONNE HUMEUR.

Ballet in one act from a comedy by Goldoni. Music by Scarlatti, orchestrated by Tommasini. Décor and costumes, Bakst. Choreography, Massine. 1918.

Vania Psota as Nicolo, the waiter.

Alexandra Danilova.

COTILLON (II).

Tamara Toumanova at the start of the amazing series of fouettés that bring the ballet to a close:

With Mother, dresser and friend. Toumanova in her dressing-room.

A holiday snap. Far from all thought of fouettés.

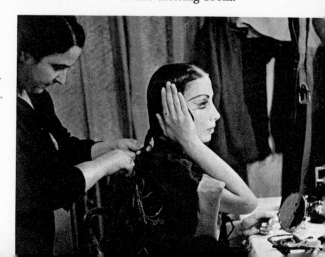

COTILLON (III).

Dance of the Hats—Harlequins, Irina Baronova, David Lichine, Olga Morosova.

A young girl (Toumanova) predicts the future.

CONCURRENCE.

Ballet by Boris Kochno. Music by Auric.
Décor and costumes, Derain. Choreography, Balanchine.

Jan Hoyer as one of the rival
shopkeepers.

Nina Verchinina in the second tableau of
Choreartium.

Anna Volkova.

Tamara Tchinarova,

Galina Razoumova.

There is no corps de ballet to-day, but an ensemble of artists, each one a potential star.

CHOREARTIUM.
Tamara Toumanova in the first movement. (*Inset*) An early rehearsal, Alhambra, 1933.

PRINCE IGOR.

Ballet to Borodin's opera.　Décor and costumes, Roerich.　Choreography, Fokine.

YUREK SHABELEVSKY.

GALA AT COVENT GARDEN.
Danilova, Massine and Baronova in a Russian dance.

END OF SEASON.
De Basil and Grigorieff discuss problems of transport

—while outside the theatre . . .

HOLIDAYS AT LAST!

1st week : " Lovely to do nothing " ;   2nd week : " Must do some exercises " ;   3rd week : " Bored, without work " ;   4th week : " Thank goodness, we dance again."